*"Daisies in water are the longest
lasting flower you can give to someone.
Fact.
Buy daisies.
Not roses."*

—American poet Anne Sexton

WAY TO GROW!

Cultivating the Weeds, Daisies, and Orchids in Your Organization

Linda Galindo

The  Company

Helping organizations achieve success through Ethical
Leadership and Values-Based Business Practices

To order additional copies of this handbook, or for information on
other WALK THE TALK® products and services,
contact us at
1.888.822.9255
or visit our website at
www.walkthetalk.com

Way To Grow!
Cultivating the Weeds, Daisies, and
Orchids in Your Organization

The WALK THE TALK Company
2925 LBJ Freeway, Suite 201
Dallas, TX 75234
972.243.8863

Printed in the United States of America
10 9 8 7 6 5 4 3 2

Printed by MultiAd®
Edited by Michelle Sedas

Contents

This book is dedicated to Sharon O'Malley at University of Maryland University College, who, underneath it all, has given me the gift of clarity and created a space for my voice to be heard.

Introduction

Choose which plant you'd most like to bring to work with you to brighten your workspace: orchid, daisy, or weed?

Would you choose the delicate orchid, with a bloom so beautiful it can soothe you, even as it takes your breath away?

Or do you prefer the daisy, whose cheerful yellow-and-white blossoms seem to bloom endlessly, no matter the season?

Who would opt to keep an ever-growing weed around the office, even one that you can't kill if your busy schedule forces you to neglect it or one that sprouts tiny, fanciful buds despite its reputation for ugliness?

Most people immediately welcome the lovely orchid. Too bad it's such a colossal pain to keep it beautiful.

Believe it or not, a busy manager like you who wants to add a bit of outdoor greenery to a drab office might be better off carting a weed to work. Weeds, after all, flourish even if you forget to water them, or even if you can't find a sunny spot near a window to leave them to do their growing. Unlike orchids, they're not picky about where they spend their time and don't need a lot of your attention—which really belongs elsewhere, anyway—to thrive.

A good second choice is the daisy, which will grow nearly as hardily as a weed with a minimal amount of fuss on your part.

Believe it or not, a busy manager who wants to add a bit of outdoor greenery to a drab office might be better off carting a weed to work.

What does this have to do with managing employees?

Think of your employees as orchids, daisies, and weeds. Think of yourself as the gardener whose job it is to nurture them to full bloom.

If you could choose the employees you'd most like to work with every day, would you select:

- Orchid employees, who need you to stick close enough to ensure they get just the right amount of—but not too much—sunlight, water, and humidity (read that: directions, feedback, and praise), or else they'll wither up and die?

- Daisy employees, who can yield voluminous blooms (excellent work) in a wide range of temperatures (situations), but still need you to check in every now and then to make sure they are getting adequate water, sunlight, and circulation (coaching, feed-back, and opportunity)?

- Or weed employees, who can fend for themselves in almost any situation, leaving you plenty of time to tend to the needier plants in the garden?

When it's put to them that way, most managers say they would welcome a garden full of weeds.

Sure, the "orchid, daisy, weed" metaphor might seem contrary; after all, we spend far too many summer weekends and way too much money trying to kill the dandelions and crab grass that grow on our lawns! We pay dearly to include the graceful orchid in our cherished bridal bouquets and prom corsages. The "orchid, daisy, weed" model turns those perceptions upside down!

Work with it. Try to equate an indestructible weed with a high-performing employee—someone who doesn't let anything stop him or her from succeeding. Compare a maintenance-hungry orchid with a low performer—someone who takes so much of your time to keep on track that you have to wonder if it's worth the effort. Using the metaphor in this way will help you understand employees, which is the first step in knowing how to allocate your *time and involvement* with them.

That's important because, unfortunately, most workplace "gardens" don't begin with a crop of ready-to-grow, impossible-to-stop, weed-like employees. Your workplace employs a diverse mixture of orchids, daisies, and weeds. As their manager, you need to identify their differences (and their differences can be vast!) and decide who needs what from you.

Chances are, you're already devoting most of your time to the *orchids*:

- New employees.

- Problem or apathetic employees.

- Employees whose skills don't quite match the job they're expected to perform.

- Employees who grew like weeds in their last positions so you promoted them to the next level ... and they're taking a while to get back up to "weed speed."

Daisies, on the other hand, can pretty much figure things out on their own. But daisies still need some coaching from you and from their more experienced peers. *Daisies* are:

- Competent employees who struggle with just a couple of their tasks.

- Employees whose lack of confidence in themselves might be keeping them from growing like high-performing weeds.

Introduction

- Otherwise exceptional workers whose personal or health problems have caused them to slip a bit on the job.

- "Weeds" who are experiencing a temporary set-back in one or two problem areas or who have taken on new responsibilities and need some time to adjust before they're performing at their peak again.

It can seem that weeds don't need you to manage them at all. *Weeds* are:

- Employees who take the next logical step without waiting for the boss to suggest it.

- Employees who get their work done well and on time.

- High performers who are eager for more responsibility and greater challenges.

The reality for you, the manager of a staff of employees whose skills are diverse, is that each one—orchid, daisy, and weed—needs you on some level. Recognizing which level of your time and involvement is necessary to help your employees bloom where they're planted—no matter what kind of flower they resemble—will help you nurture each one appropriately and effectively.

Way To Grow!

This book will help you sort your employees out. It will help you determine who needs your time and why. It will help you decide how much time to spend with each orchid, daisy, and weed to maximize his or her chances for on-the-job success.

On these pages, you will find:

- Guidelines for categorizing your employees as needy orchids, potentially great daisies, or unstoppable weeds.

- Hints for determining how much time and involvement you, as a manager, should give to each type of employee.

- Tips for effectively coaching orchids and daisies in a way that will help them grow into the most desirable office plant: the weed.

- Insight that will help you engage, as a manager and coach, with a weed who might seem to be doing fine without any feedback from you.

- Food for thought about what kind of employee *you* are, and suggestions for those times when you might need some help finding your way back to the weed garden.

The success of your orchids, daisies, and weeds, of course, is part of *your* success and your organization's success. The gardener will be judged by the health and beauty of the garden.

Read, learn, and apply these lessons. Then watch your garden grow!

"Whatever you are, be a good one."

—Abraham Lincoln

"Only I can change my life.
No one can do it for me."

—*Carol Burnett*

The Garden of Empowerment

A great myth in the American workplace is that a manager can empower an employee to succeed.

It just isn't so.

Empowerment means taking action and facing risk in order to get what you want. It's the way to ensure that you achieve the result you want.

Nobody but you can take action and face risk to get what you want. Nobody but you can decide whether the risks are worth the potential payoff. Nobody but you can decide if your environment is a safe place to take those risks.

There is only one person who can empower an employee, and that's the employee.

So how can you, as a manager, do that for somebody else?

You can't.

There is only one person who can empower an employee, and that's the employee. There is only one kind of empowerment, and that's self-empowerment.

Empowered employees take risks. They:
- **Realize** that their results are the consequences of their own choices.
- **If** it is to be, it's up to me. This is their mantra.
- **Step** out of their comfort zones.
- **Keep** focused.

You can't have empowerment without personal responsibility and personal accountability. Empowerment involves a mindset of ownership and personal responsibility for one's actions. It involves a mindset that something needs to be different and a determination to do whatever it takes in order to make it different. People empower themselves, take actions, accept the risk, make change happen—and then answer for the result.

In other words, empowered people:

1. Take responsibility for the success or failure of their choices, behaviors, and actions—*before* they know how it all turns out. They own all of it, even if they're working for somebody else or as part of a team.

2. Empower *themselves* to succeed. They take the actions and the risks that they need to in order to achieve the results they desire.

3. Are accountable for those actions. They show that they are willing to answer for the outcomes that result from their choices, behaviors, and actions.

The Garden of Empowerment

In the Garden of Empowerment, empowered employees are called *weeds*.

Weeds are low-maintenance employees. Managers don't have to tend to them or water them or tell them how to get from one side of a cement sidewalk to the other—they just figure it out. These weed-employees perform well even if their busy managers ignore them. If you give them a clear, end-point description, you can count on them to meet your expectations. It's as if they can read your mind, and you love having them around.

The 85 Percent Solution

Weed-employees believe that at least 85 percent of their success on any given day or any given project depends on themselves and on nothing else—not how much it rains or whether the landscaper is coming that day with a vat of weed killer to clean up the garden. They don't complain that their teammates aren't pulling their weight or that they get stuck with all the boring jobs. Still, they're not so naive as to believe there are no barriers to their success; indeed, weeds will ask you where the weed killer is so they can make a plan for getting out of its way. They don't blame the weed killer for their setbacks.

Most managers are lucky enough to have at least a couple of weeds on staff. But most also have to deal with the weed's polar opposite: orchid-employees.

Most managers are lucky enough to have at least a couple of weeds on staff. But most also have to deal with the

weed's polar opposite: *orchid*-employees, who blame
failure, mistakes, and missed opportunities on everyone
but themselves. Orchids believe that they are responsible
for very little of their own success. To them, factors
beyond their control—like a coworker's actions, a
supervisor's attitude, a lack of resources, or simple bad
luck—determine how the project will turn out.

While the weed is an "85–15," the orchid might be a
"50–50." Half of their success is up to them, and half,
they believe, isn't. Daisies fall in between: Daisy-
employees believe that they determine 70 percent to
80 percent of their success, but that outside factors are
responsible for up to 30 percent of it.

Which are you?

Your response to the following question will reveal a lot
about you: *How much of your success is up to you, and
how much of it is determined by outside conditions, like
the environment, other people, or just plain bad luck?*

Forty percent you, 60 percent environment? Half and half?
One hundred percent you, forget the outside world?

What your answer reveals is how successful a person
you are.

  • If you answered 85 percent (or higher) *you*, 15 percent
    (or less) *outside conditions*, that says you believe that
    you see yourself as mostly responsible for your own

success. (Congratulations, you're a weed!) And you're probably a successful person.

• On the other hand, if you answered 50–50 or anywhere less than 85–15, be honest: Are you as successful as you would like to be? Or do other people, situations, and influences seem to always stand in the way of your getting ahead?

A Daily Decision

Suppose you manage two employees who work at exactly the same job. As Employee A walks out of his house in the morning, he believes that 60 percent of the success of the day's work belongs to him, and 40 percent depends on outside conditions: the boss's mood; how often the telephone rings; whether he gets a flat tire on the way to work; how well he slept the night before.

His coworker, Employee B, on the other hand, is more optimistic about her chances for success. She's pretty sure that 85 percent of her success depends on her, and just 15 percent will be motivated by outside sources.

It should come as no surprise that, when quitting time rolls around, Employee B has had a more productive and happier day than Employee A. Maybe Employee B ignored the boss's bad mood, or figured out a way to cheer him up and engage him in the task at hand. Perhaps she chose not to answer the telephone for two hours so she could work without interruptions and finish her project quicker. And because she slept poorly the night before, she compensated by taking a brisk walk at lunchtime instead of sitting in the too warm cafeteria, becoming over-relaxed, and eating the comfort foods that she knows can make her sleepy. When she noticed that one of her car's tires looked low on air that morning, she swung by the service station and had them take a look—and sure enough, the mechanic found a slow leak and changed the tire. She took charge of her situation, her day, her progress, and her success. She decided before she left the house in the morning that she was responsible—at least 85 percent of the way—for the success of her own day.

In short, she decided before she left the house that she would have a successful day, and so she had one.

She's a weed.

That kind of attitude is available to everyone. Employees who believe that they are at least 85 percent responsible for their success—and that just 15 percent of the success of a project or a day depends on the way the wind blows—will get the results they're looking for.

The most unstoppable weeds believe that 100 percent of their success is up to them and zero is influenced by outside conditions.

> *Employees who believe that they are at least 85 percent responsible for their success will get the results they're looking for.*

The Garden of Empowerment

An employee's mindset determines how much responsibility she will take for her success. And for better or worse, she decides that *before* she begins her work. *She* determines her level of achievement in advance.

Nobody—even the best manager—can make that decision for an employee. You can't force an employee to take responsibility for how a job turns out. You can't force your employees to empower themselves to make sure their work turns out well.

If you try, you could find yourself too embroiled in work you should be delegating—and trusting employees to do.

To orchids, that's just fine. If you do more, they can do less.

Manage-Level Versus Coach-Level

Orchid-employees need extra care and attention: special food, moist soil, lots of humidity (extra supervision, more hand-holding, frequent discipline). Orchids suck the resources right out of you. They are high-maintenance.

Orchid-employees are "manage-level" people.

It's appropriate for brand-new employees to be orchids; with some time and coaching, they turn into daisies with the potential to become weeds. But some orchid-employees never blossom into daisies. They have

The most unstoppable weeds believe that 100 percent of their success is up to them and zero is influenced by outside conditions.

been on the job for a long time and still need to touch base with the supervisor every day, don't work independently, whine about the work, and steal time from managers and coworkers because they need so much help and attention to do their jobs.

These bad orchids drain the organization's resources and, sadly, need to be dug up and transplanted in jobs that suit them better—sometimes in other organizations.

Orchids do not empower themselves to succeed at work.

Orchids do not empower themselves to succeed at work. Perhaps they don't want to work very hard. But more likely:

1. They're unclear about what is expected of them.

2. They are unable to gain the authority they need to carry out their projects.

3. They are frozen with fear because their boss constantly criticizes their work.

In response, they fall short on the job.

It is very expensive to run an organization if you have to tell your employees what to do, then check on them to see that they did it, or hire people to check on them. It's far better to set clear expectations and practice a little bit of patience so your employees can ask all of their questions and know for sure what is expected of them. Then the boss can let them get to work, knowing that all parties are on the same page.

Setting clear expectations for employees helps them maximize their ownership of the project at hand. It makes it easier for them to empower themselves to take the actions—including taking risks and making tough decisions—that are necessary in order to get the job done according to their understanding of your expectations.

In fact, managers cannot be too clear when it comes to letting employees know what they expect from them. Making yourself perfectly clear takes five steps:

1. Tell the employee exactly what you want. Do not expect anyone to read your mind!

2. Ask the employee to explain your expectations in his or her own words. Some will balk at this, saying it's unnecessary, but insist on it.

3. Ask if the employee agrees to do what you have asked, according to the expectations you've explained.

4. Explain what the consequence will be if the employee fails to fulfill the agreement.

5. Enforce that consequence if the employee doesn't hold up the agreement.

With weeds, you probably can skip Steps 2 through 5. With most orchids, though, you'll need to follow the process strictly.

Although you cannot empower your employees, you can create an environment that encourages them to empower themselves. Setting clear expectations is a key to creating that environment.

Planting daisy-employees in an environment of empowerment works especially well. Daisies are "coach-level" workers; that is, they have the potential to grow and produce like weeds, but they need a little push now and then. Some daisies are drought-resistant: They just need watering now and then. That sort of employee might need coaching once a month for an hour for three months before transforming into a high-performing weed. Another daisy might need extra shade plus lots of water—the equivalent of coaching twice a month for six months. More delicate daisies might need water, shade for part of the day, and sun in the afternoons; they are barely more independent than orchids. Those equivalent employees might need lots of attention from supervisors for extended times or they won't survive, and in fact, they might never "bloom" into weeds.

So you can see that it's not practical to devote the same amount of time to every employee, and in fact, it's not even fair.

Creating an environment of empowerment means giving people what they need to thrive. A weed is no better than an orchid; it's just different. It has different needs. If you treat a weed like an orchid, you'll kill it, and vice versa. Managers need to determine what each employee needs to grow and perform well, and supply that.

Micromanagers who believe in treating everyone the same for equity's sake will never grow their organization into an environment of empowerment.

The truth is: No manager has time to devote an equal amount of attention to every employee. Supervisors need to focus on coaching the ones with the potential to grow into weeds.

Still, orchids need more coaching and supervision than weeds, so bosses wind up spending more time with the orchids. That's appropriate. The key is to focus on the employee's needs and to be patient enough to devote the time it requires to get that employee to the point at which he or she no longer requires so much of the boss's time.

Creating an environment of empowerment means giving people what they need to thrive.

Managers can more effectively parcel out their time to employees if they classify them as needy orchids, high-potential daisies, or independent weeds. Knowing what kind of employee you're dealing with can direct you to allocate the appropriate amount of time and involvement to each one.

Way To Grow!

"*Weeds are not supposed to grow,*
But by degrees
Some achieve a flower, although
No one sees."

—British poet Philip Larkin

Way To Grow!

Weeds, Daisies, and Orchids
Don't Kill the Weeds!

Just as your intuition might tell you that a fragile orchid would make a better office plant than an unruly weed, you might think it's easier to manage a weed-employee than an orchid-employee.

Both assumptions would be wrong.

Workplace weeds are, in so many ways, a manager's dream come true. They're smart, quick, dedicated, and responsible. They are mightily empowered to succeed— by their own positive attitudes and self-accountability.

Therein lies the manager's dilemma: Supervisors are apt to ignore weed-employees because they seem to perform just as well without any interference from the boss. In fact, it can be awkward to try to coach employees who are already performing at the top of their game.

So don't. Remember: Orchids, daisies, and weeds are different kinds of employees and need different things from their managers:

Manage orchids.
Coach daisies.
Lead weeds.

Still, all employees, no matter how bright or independent, crave feedback and at least a modicum of attention. Employees of all skill levels like to be complimented on a job well done and reminded that their hard work is being noticed and appreciated.

With weeds, though, less is more when it comes to the manager's time and involvement. Like the leafy weed in a backyard garden, the weed-employees' sprawling growth and resourcefulness are very much the product of their being left on their own to figure out how to thrive in any situation.

In fact, weeds will let the manager know how much attention to give them.

Here's how to spot the weeds among your employees.

Weeds:

• Embrace each chore—large or small—as important and worthy of their best work.

• Figure out how to complete each job successfully. If they need it, they'll ask for help, but not until they've tried to solve the dilemma on their own. When they ask questions, the queries inevitably show they have put some thought into the task at hand.

• Display a positive attitude about work and life. They rarely complain.

Weeds, Daisies, and Orchids

- Finish on time. Or they finish early and seek extra duties. You won't catch them sneaking out early or goofing off just because they've completed the day's assignment.

- Take pride in their work.

- Welcome new opportunities and extra responsibility.

Managing Weeds

Employees with those remarkable attributes need very little from their supervisors in terms of instructions, supervision, or discipline. So it might seem that they have little need for their managers at all.

That's not necessarily true. While managers can—and should—spend far less time and become way less involved with a weed than with a can't-do-anything-alone orchid, the weed still needs leadership, praise for a job well done, and new challenges.

The manager of a weed, then, should *lead the weed* rather than try to manage the weed. Set a good example, show your trust and confidence, pat your weeds on the back—and then move out of their way!

> *The manager of a weed should lead the weed rather than try to manage the weed.*

33

How to Lead a Weed

1. **Offer regular feedback**—at least once a month. Point out exactly what your high-performing weeds are doing right, so they will continue to do it. Still, even if all you have to say is, "Good job!" be assured that your weed-employees will be glad to hear it. Throw in a "Thank you!" every now and then, too. Every employee likes to feel appreciated. Weeds treasure handwritten thank-you notes from the boss.

2. **Offer your weeds greater challenges**. They will embrace them as opportunities to grow, use their considerable skills, and "strut their stuff." Assign tasks that these employees can complete on their own.

3. **Step aside**. Let the weeds figure their new tasks out on their own. They're not the kind of workers who need you to spell everything out, step by step. If they need your help, they'll ask for it. If they need more feedback, they'll say so. Weeds are employees who make it their mission to accomplish their goals, and they take full responsibility for gathering the information, tools, and resources they need to make that happen.

Managing by leading makes some managers uncomfortable. These managers believe that employees aren't working if a manager can't see them working, or that they're not doing the job right if they're not doing it exactly as the manager would do it.

But employees who are given the tools they need to empower themselves do not need to be micromanaged or controlled; in fact, they will not perform at their peak if they are. Managers need to empower *themselves* to trust employees who have demonstrated that they deserve that trust. They should delegate tasks— important, challenging tasks that allow their weeds to work independently—and provide the necessary resources. Then they should let those employees do their jobs.

In other words, trust your weeds! You know they are people who deliver what they promise. They've earned your trust already; that's how you know they're weeds.

Sure, stepping aside is a risk for the manager, who has to count on the employee to do the work well and on time. It's also a risk for the employee, who has to work hard and smart enough to meet the manager's expectations. But empowered employees take risks if they need to in order to get the job done.

> *Trust your weeds!*
> *They've earned it.*

Wildflowers

Some weeds are so good at their jobs and so confident of their abilities that they don't know their own limits. This means it's important for managers to be involved with them just enough to spot signs of trouble.

Here's an example from a nursing manager at a large hospital who had to prune one of her weeds:

This weed, a registered nurse who specializes in ambulatory care, is an "outstanding, wonderful clinician," the nursing manager explains. Patients love her. She's been on the job longer than many of the physicians she works with. She is so bright and educated that often, when she suggests treatments or medications for patients, the doctors authorize them. Sometimes, the docs even ask her for her opinion.

She believes she knows enough to prescribe these treatments and medicines on her own. Still, her nursing license prohibits her from doing that. In fact, it's against the law for her to administer treatments and drugs without a doctor's orders.

Every now and then, she does it anyway if it's a very small procedure or dose. She knows a doctor eventually will sign off on it; she's always on target with her diagnoses. If she waits for the doctor's order, the treatment could be delayed, the patient could suffer longer than necessary, and the case will remain open.

The nurse would rather have it finished. (She's a weed, after all, and eager to resolve this challenge and tackle her next one.)

The nurse manager doesn't want to snip this weed's stem, but she also doesn't want her breaking the law. So she makes her expectations absolutely clear to the nurse and instructs her to get a doctor's order before administering treatments or drugs.

A manager who did not pay any attention to the weeds in her care might never have known about the nurse's actions, and wouldn't have had a chance to stop them before someone got in trouble—or worse, before a patient was injured.

Gone to Seed

It's not uncommon for weeds to occasionally backslide into the daisy patch, or even to slip, very temporarily, into the orchid garden. Most of the time, this happens when a weed does so well in one job that the manager transplants the weed to a position of more responsibility or changes the weed's job altogether with the hope of spreading that can-do attitude to an area that needs help.

It's not reasonable to expect an employee—even a stellar employee like a weed—to deliver a perfect, expert performance the first day, week, or month on a new job. An employee who is highly skilled and productive as a technician might not have a clue how to manage other technicians, but that doesn't mean the employee won't grow into an outstanding manager with the right coaching.

Weeds-turned-daisies have the same need as daisies for regularly scheduled coaching.

Weeds-turned-daisies have the same need as daisies for regularly scheduled coaching on specific issues for as long as it takes to gear the employee back up to "weed speed." Because weeds work hard and learn quickly, that usually doesn't take very long.

Likewise, some weeds take on new responsibilities that are so great that they revert to uncertain orchids. While this regression is temporary, the weeds-turned-orchids need their managers to treat them accordingly while they're in this delicate state. Managers of these onetime weeds should oversee their work and offer extra feedback,

Weeds, Daisies, and Orchids

at least until the employee gets the hang of the new job. Again, it shouldn't take long.

In fact, most weeds welcome the chance to take a step back—to become a daisy or even an orchid—if it means they get to learn something new, prepare for a promotion, or take on more challenging work. Weeds, even when they're paying a temporary visit to the daisy patch, seek and respond to training and invite coaching when they feel they need it. And they're not shy about letting their managers know when they need it.

Still, weeds-turned-daisies and weeds-turned-orchids remain, at their core, weeds. When weeds take on more or unfamiliar responsibilities, the manager should allow them to figure out how to do the task in a way that's best for them. Trust that they will bring a weed's work ethic to the new position. Remember: Weeds believe that they are at least 85 percent responsible for making their own success.

An empowered employee, even one who needs some extra training or coaching, will figure out how to get the job done without demanding much from the manager.

Way To Grow!

"The rose has but a summer's reign;
the daisy never dies."

—Scottish poet James Montgomery

Way To Grow!

Weeds, Daisies, and Orchids
Pushing Up Daisies

"Daisy, Daisy, give me your
answer, do ..."

—From "Bicycle Built for Two"

What an appropriate theme song for the in-between daisy, which can bloom all day every day for a year with barely a drop of water or a glint of sunlight ... or do just the opposite: wilt, shrivel, and die from neglect!

Which will your workplace daisies be: the hardy, independent variety, or the kind who depend on you, their gardener, for every breath? (Give me your answer, do!)

Here's the reality: It's largely up to you. You can push your daisies up (into the weed garden) or keep them down.

Daisy-employees have so much potential. They're weeds-in-waiting, yet some don't ever reach the wonderful world of weeds.

The ones who don't reach their potential most likely have not received the necessary time and involvement from busy managers who believed the hardy flowers to be enough like weeds that they could let their daisies fend for themselves.

It's no surprise that managers so often miscalculate the amount of time and involvement that their daisies require. It's because there are so many varieties of daisies, so it can be difficult to determine what each one needs from a manager.

That miscalculation reinforces the importance of identifying employees as independent weeds, high-potential daisies, or needy orchids. It's not uncommon for a manager to misidentify a daisy as a weed because daisies are usually smart and able employees who have more than their share of "weed moments." But when managers lump daisies into the wrong category, they rob their rising stars of the opportunity to shine as brightly as possible.

Daisies are "coach-level" employees. They don't need the same intense, hands-on management that the fragile orchid demands. Nor can a boss "manage by leading" a daisy as often or as completely as is possible with a self-sufficient weed.

> *Daisies need regular coaching that usually is temporary and is focused on a few areas of weakness.*

Instead, daisies need something in between: regular coaching that usually is temporary and is focused on a few areas of

Weeds, Daisies, and Orchids

weakness. With the proper coaching from you or from an experienced coworker you entrust with the job, those daisies soon transform into weeds and will demand less of your time and involvement. Without the proper coaching, well ... *isn't your orchid garden full enough?*

How can you tell a daisy from an orchid or a weed?

Daisies:

- Live up to their potential, for the most part.

- Take initiative at work without waiting for the manager to give them step-by-step instructions. If they need instructions, they'll ask for them.

- Can articulate where their interests and strengths lie.

- Are responsive to training and coaching and, in fact, seek it out.

- Are receptive to feedback, and often ask for it.

- Require a *moderate* amount of time and involvement from their managers, usually on specific trouble spots.

- Often become independent weeds after a period of targeted coaching.

A Doozy of a Daisy

If you treat daisy-employees like orchids— by hovering too closely with too specific instructions, too frequent check-ins, and too careful monitoring— you'll suffocate them.

The manager of the Information Technology Department at a large organization tells how that nearly happened to one of her daisy-employees, but she intervened just in time.

The employee, an entry-level telephone operator on the help desk at a call center, stayed in that job for five years, growing from a new-on-the-job orchid to a competent, confident daisy. Some would have called him a weed, as he outperformed most of his coworkers and demonstrated he had the potential for bigger and better things. But the call center manager continually coached him to keep his enthusiasm in check; in short, she treated him like an orchid and nearly prevented him from growing into a weed.

The employee was waiting for a more responsible position to open up elsewhere in the department so he could apply for it, but none had.

Because most of the help desk's operators are young employees who have not held prior jobs and have no formal IT training, the call center manager watches them very closely. She often listens in on their calls and lets them know how she would have handled their callers differently. She insists that they work from a uniform script, so that they're all giving the same advice to solve the same dilemmas. She tells them how many callers she expects them to help each hour. She leaves nothing up to their creativity and does not expect them to take any initiative.

So most don't.

This particular daisy did. He helped more callers than anyone, often by drawing on his years of help desk experience to offer useful advice that would resolve their problems quickly, even though that advice wasn't in the script. He took it upon himself to help his coworkers when they fielded unusually tough calls. And he let his manager know he was ready to move on.

The call center manager responded by scolding him for taking initiative. She told him to stick to the script and let the manager intervene when coworkers needed help.

Once the daisy came to the attention of the department manager, however, it wasn't long before he was promoted to a more challenging position.

"He was a weed in an orchid garden," notes the department manager, who arranged to have a job created for him rather than make him wait any longer for someone to quit or retire.

Today, that onetime daisy is a full-grown weed in his new position, having retained daisy status for no more than three weeks into the new job. "He just totally took off," the department manager says. "I knew he had the initiative."

And the department manager admonishes others: If that employee were not a weed at heart, he might have responded to the call center manager's treatment by behaving like an orchid—because he was being treated like one.

Weeds, Daisies, and Orchids

A Daisy Bouquet

Daisies come in so many varieties that it's hard to pigeon-hole them into a single category.

Some are so hardy that they can thrive in drought-like conditions. Likewise, some daisy-employees will do just fine if their manager neglects them, even for an extended time.

Several varieties of the cheerful perennial can tolerate the frost, but extreme cold will kill others. And while some daisy strains soak up the sun during severely hot days, others will bake to death under the very same hot sun.

Their employee counterparts have their idiosyncrasies as well. Some can stand the heat, so to speak, while others shrink under pressure.

When a manager classifies an employee as a daisy, it's important to dig a little deeper to assign the employee to a subcategory.

Doing this will help you determine how much time to spend coaching each daisy-employee. Although they're all daisies, you can't treat them all the same.

A useful measure for dividing your daisies is the *accountability scale.*

It's hard to pigeonhole daisies into a single category.

Way To Grow!

Ask them this question: On a scale from zero to 100, how much of your success depends on you, and how much of it depends on something or someone else, like your coworkers, your boss, or your personal life?

Weeds, you'll recall, accept at least 85 percent of the responsibility for their success, and blame no more than 15 percent on anyone or anything else.

Daisies, on the other hand, will give answers like 71 percent *me*, 29 percent *outside conditions*. Or 78 percent *me*, 22 percent *outside conditions*. They're not quite ready for the weed world, whose members empower themselves to succeed through an attitude of high accountability and personal responsibility.

And while there are hundreds of varieties of the *Bellis Perennis*, or Day's Eye—just as there can be thousands of unique employee personalities in every organization—you can map your plan for coaching by dividing your workplace daisies into three broad categories. Let's call them drought-resistant daisies, shade-loving daisies, and hybrid daisies.

Weeds, Daisies, and Orchids

Coaching Daisies

Drought-resistant daisies

Drought-resistant daisy-employees are high-performing and weed-like. Once you get them planted, soak them thoroughly with the education, tools, and resources they need to do their jobs, and see that they're firmly established, it's not long before they take off—well, like weeds. They might be high performers whose progress is slowed by a single trouble spot, or onetime weeds who are feeling a little overwhelmed by new responsibilities.

Drought-resistant daisies typically take around 78 percent of the responsibility for their own success. That means they leave 22 percent up to the weather. They're good, but they're not 85–15 weeds.

> *It's important to remember that the daisy—even a daisy with lots of weed potential—is not yet a weed. It's a flower.*

Indeed, it's important to remember that the daisy—even a daisy with lots of weed potential—is not yet a weed. It's a flower. As such, it needs a bit more care and feeding than an indestructible weed.

Coaching a drought-resistant daisy takes very little time, but the task deserves the manager's utmost attention. Employees who mimic this hardy strain are the organization's up-and-coming weeds. They're the manager's best hope for expanding the weed garden, as their stay in the daisy patch is usually temporary—just long enough to get up to speed after taking on new responsibilities or to work through a specific work-related trouble spot.

The manager of a drought-resistant daisy-employee should dedicate about an hour of uninterrupted, one-on-one time to this sort of daisy once a month for three months. By the end of that time, it will be clear whether the daisy is going to take off like a weed or move to a place in the patch with less promising daisies who may need more intense coaching before they can bloom to their full potential.

Shade-loving daisies

Shade-loving daisy-employees can be confounding. They're capable and competent and their managers believe they *should* be thriving—but something seems to be holding them back. Shade-loving daisies could be, for example, mature workers whose many years of experience and impressive knowledge of their work make them indispensable, but they're stumped by the new technology that they're suddenly expected to use on the job. Or they could be expert technicians who have been tapped, because of their success and skill, to teach or lead others—but have never been teachers or leaders before.

In either case, they have great potential to excel despite the changes they face—but not without their manager's help.

Still, shade-loving daisies will admit that they take only around 75 percent of the responsibility for their success. They attribute a full quarter of it, then, to factors beyond their control.

Weeds, Daisies, and Orchids

Managers of shade-loving daisies often enlist the help of other staff members in bringing these high-potential employees up to "weed speed." A manager, for example, might pair a mature worker with a fresh college graduate who grew up using computers and can demonstrate the new technology and answer the daisy's specific questions about it. Or the manager might invite a seasoned trainer to mentor the expert technician-turned-educator until the daisy gains enough confidence to teach those skills to others.

Shade-loving daisies often need this sort of one-on-one coaching twice a month in digestible, hour-long sessions with the tutor/mentor/colleague. The formal arrangement might last for six months or until the daisy demonstrates a mastery of the problem area.

Hybrid daisies

Hybrid daisies border on the delicate, but they're not as fragile as orchids. Still, they need considerably more time and involvement from their managers in order to move up the daisy chain and establish themselves among the hardier varieties.

Employees who fit in this category might be, for example, new supervisors who have accepted promotions that landed them in charge of the people who used to be their peers. (This kind of promotion, while an honor, can blow the petals right off of any flower's capitulum. Suddenly, they're required to hold their friends accountable for their work and behavior. That's a hard transition for anyone.)

Way To Grow!

Hybrid daisies rank a bit low on the accountability scale. Ask them how much of their success is solely up to them, and they're likely to hover around 71 percent. They'll admit that a full 29 percent has nothing to do with them.

Such an employee is still a skilled and competent worker, but needs *a lot* of help adjusting to the new role or level of responsibility. *That help should come in the form of coaching directly from the manager in the form of thrice-monthly, hour-long meetings for about three months, or until the new supervisor feels comfortable ending the sessions.*

> *Hybrid daisies rank a bit low on the accountability scale.*

In all cases, of course, the manager and employee might agree that the worker should also attend training classes or other educational events that can help with the transition.

Coaching Daisies

Managers who want to transplant daisies into the weed garden can:

- Determine, with input from the employee, where the daisy's trouble spots are.

- Schedule regular meetings of about an hour with the daisy to work on specific areas that need improvement. The frequency of those meetings— and the number of weeks or months they continue— will depend on the employee's progress.

- Keep every appointment with the daisy. Make the coaching sessions a priority. Daisy-employees frequently demonstrate weed-like potential, yet they're still flowers and need committed care from the manager—at least temporarily.

- Don't treat daisies like orchids. They're more independent and capable, and need less hand-holding and monitoring. Over-managing daisies can turn them into orchids (or prompt them to look for new positions and new managers to treat them more appropriately).

- Let your daisy-employees tell you when they've had enough coaching. They'll let you know when they're ready to go it on their own.

Way To Grow!

"Do you like orchids? ... Nasty things. Their flesh is too much like the flesh of men, and their perfume has the rotten sweetness of corruption."

—From "The Big Sleep" (1946)

Way To Grow!

Weeds, Daisies, and Orchids
Orchids and Their Opposites

They say beauty is only skin-deep. That may be the case
with the irresistible orchid.

The flower's visible beauty is perfect, breathtaking …
but it needs massive maintenance in order to stay that way.
The gardener who cares for the gentle blossom does so
painstakingly, devoting more time to it than to many of
the other plants in the garden or greenhouse.

To neglect those other plants because the orchid demands
so much of the gardener's time could be that caretaker's
downfall. It could also be the downfall of the rest of the
plants in the garden, or of the garden itself.

So gardeners whose fields include delicate orchids must
pace themselves, and make wise decisions about how
much time to spend with the fragile flowers and how much
to devote to the rest of the floral crop.

The same is true for the manager whose staff includes
orchid-employees. Orchid-employees typically fall into
one of two categories:

- Employees who are brand-new to an organization or to a position that requires vastly different skills from their previous jobs.

- Career orchids, or employees who will never advance beyond their current positions because of a lack of skill, ambition, or accountability.

Orchid-employees can monopolize the manager's time to the peril of the daisies and even the weeds.

Both kinds of orchids need massive amounts of the manager's time: the first in order to succeed; the second in order to maintain the status quo.

Orchid-employees of either stripe can monopolize the manager's time to the peril of the daisies and even the weeds who also are that manager's responsibility.

Yet many orchids, once the manager has committed the time and resources to helping them flourish, grow into high-performing weeds in no time.

So the manager has to decide, on an employee-by-employee basis, whether devoting large quantities of time to one-on-one managing is going to pay off for the organization.

Knowing which kind of orchid you're dealing with is the manager's first step in deciding how much time and involvement to devote to an orchid-employee.

Weeds, Daisies, and Orchids

Double Blooms

Most orchid-employees need special time and attention from their managers for just a few weeks or months after joining a new organization or accepting a new job that requires skills beyond the employee's experience.

Those brand-new employees need to get established: to learn the organization's culture, to practice doing things the way they're done in your department, or to work with mentors and trainers until they acquire the necessary skills and are comfortable using them on the job. They need time to ask questions; to understand where their authority lies; and to clarify their role and responsibilities.

They usually reveal themselves as capable daisies or unstoppable weeds within a few weeks or months, and the manager can "transplant" them to a "coach-level" (for daisies) or "manage-by-leading" (for weeds) relationship.

> *Managers of career orchids can cite a never-ending list of their symptoms.*

The ones who do not show the same promise in fairly short order, however, might never grow into hardy daisies or independent weeds. They'll always be orchids: fragile, delicate, and time-consuming. Managers of these career orchids can cite a never-ending list of their symptoms.

Way To Grow!

Career orchids:

- Are high-maintenance. They take things too literally. Their managers need to fully explain what they want and exactly how the employee is to accomplish it. If anything is unclear, the orchid cannot—or will not—proceed with the assignment.

- Do not try to clarify areas of confusion if the confusion means they'll get out of work or will benefit them in some other way.

- Get others to do their work for them. Coworkers and even managers often figure it's easier and quicker to do the work themselves than to take the time to hold an orchid's hand through the whole job or hold them accountable for doing it well and on time.

- Appear to lack an emotional investment in the work or in their relationships with coworkers and managers.

- Refuse to acknowledge their responsibility for an outcome—especially a bad one. They blame others for their failures, even when others can see a clear connection between those failures and the orchid's coming late to work, missing deadlines, or slacking on the job.

Both kinds of orchids are "manage-level" employees. *Both need to touch base with the manager on a daily basis until they grow enough to work more independently.* The meetings may be as brief as 15 minutes a day, or may last for several hours, depending on how much help and instruction the employee needs.

Weeds, Daisies, and Orchids

By working closely with an orchid, the manager can identify any shortfalls in the employee's skills or capabilities. During the daily meetings, the manager should specifically address those shortfalls.

By working closely with an orchid, the manager can identify any shortfalls in the employee's skills or capabilities.

The objective of the meetings is to get the orchid onto a solid *growth plan* that will allow the employee to chart his or her own performance and growth, under the manager's guidance.

Managing Orchids

During daily meetings with orchid-employees, managers should:

- Teach, clarify, and discuss *specific* areas that appear to be weaknesses or concerns of the employee.

- Praise the employee's strengths and successes. Reassure orchids that they are worth the time and effort that you're devoting to them.

- Offer feedback about the employee's performance since the last meeting. Allow time for the orchid to ask questions and address concerns.

- Schedule a time for the next meeting—and stick to it.

While the manager's time and involvement with the orchid is considerable, it's almost always worth it. Most orchids grow to be more self-reliant, and as they do, they need far less of your time.

A Tale of Two Orchids

The owner of a small publishing company had opposite experiences with two young orchid-employees whom she hired (the second after the first one didn't work out) to do the same job.

The job description: An editorial assistant who can do Internet research and telephone interviews to collect information for articles; who can write well and quickly; who doesn't mind pitching in on the occasional typing/envelope-stuffing project; and who is a careful proofreader.

Assistant #1 seemed like a dream when she took the job. She was friendly to her coworkers, asked lots of good questions of her manager and of those she interviewed for articles, had a pleasant telephone manner, and always came to work on time. She was honest, never goofed off, and seemed to love her work.

That is ... until the manager began to point out the many errors she was making: misspelled names, multiple typos in documents that were to be published, rampant grammatical and sentence-structure errors, and careless proofreading. And when it came to typing and stuffing envelopes, Assistant #1 was unreasonably slow and complained that the publisher should assign that tedious work to someone else.

Weeds, Daisies, and Orchids

The manager began to meet with the employee at the end of each workday. Every day for a month, she thanked Assistant #1 for the things she did well (her excellent telephone manner and interviewing skills were an asset, for sure). But the manager also pointed out the many errors Assistant #1 made and offered suggestions for how the employee could improve her performance.

In response, Assistant #1 cried. She said she was doing her best. She blamed the manager for the problem, saying none of her former bosses had ever complained about her work.

In short, she refused to take responsibility for any of her errors. Without accepting personal responsibility, there was no way she could empower herself to work more carefully and make fewer errors. It was as if she refused to improve.

The manager had no choice but to replace her; a publisher can't tolerate a careless employee. Mistakes that are printed are permanent!

Assistant #2 seemed like a dream at first, too, but the once-burned, twice-shy manager wasn't assuming it would last. Starting his first day on the job, she met with him for 15 minutes at the end of every workday. She praised him for his energy, his excellent interviewing skills, and his beautiful writing. He told her how much he wanted to succeed and asked her for specific feedback on his work.

By the end of the second week, the manager knew she could stop the daily briefings. Assistant #2 came to her as an orchid in full bloom, happy and thriving, ready to transform himself—and needing little from the manager except the opportunity to do it—directly into a weed. And he did.

Assistant #2 has been a weed ever since.

Transplanting Orchids

Orchid-employees can go in one of three directions:

- Upward and onward, to the daisy patch or weed garden, where they can showcase their abilities and talents with just a bit of coaching and smart leadership from their managers.

- Out the door, to jobs that suit them better. Usually, this means they leave the company because their poor performance and stunted growth haven't earned them a permanent spot.

- Nowhere at all. Career orchids often languish in the same jobs for years, either because the manager does not want to deal with the unpleasantness that surrounds documenting and acting on poor performance or, in some cases, because the manager can't pinpoint a specific infraction that would make the orchid worthy of termination.

Orchids who show no potential (or desire) to grow and move up probably never will.

Orchids who show no potential (or desire) to grow and move up, even after months of extensive, one-on-one management, probably never will. Managers who opt to keep them can try one of two tactics:

- Continue to pour fruitless hours of time into trying to transform this orchid-for-life into a higher-performing daisy, and rob other staff members of your time and attention in the process.

- Leave such orchids to their own devices, and hope for the best. In rare cases, an orchid whose manager suddenly stops calling the employee into the office for meetings or discipline actually will shape up for fear that the change of behavior means a pink slip will soon follow. It's more likely, though, that unchecked orchids will continue their poor performance and disruptive behavior, which can cause morale and productivity problems all around.

What do you do when a career orchid believes he or she is a weed?

Ask yourself a simple question: *Does the employee meet job expectations?* If your honest answer is "no," ask yourself another question: *Why is that employee still working for you?*

Your most responsible option once you identify a career orchid is to begin the process to remove the orchid from the garden: following the organization's prescribed policies for documenting performance and behavior; making reasonable efforts to help the employee improve; finally, terminating the orchid.

An unruly orchid can choke the life out of the daisies and weeds who have to work around that low-performing employee in order to do their jobs.

Weeds, Daisies, and Orchids

To take the "weed, daisy, orchid" metaphor to its extreme, consider this: An unruly orchid can choke the life out of the daisies and weeds who have to work around that low-performing employee in order to do their jobs.

Sometimes it's better to sacrifice one flower for the good of all the weeds in the garden.

Way To Grow!

*"Action springs not from thought,
but from a readiness for
responsibility."*

*—Theologian and author
Dietrich Bonhoeffer*

Way To Grow!

The Good Gardener

As you put the "weed, daisy, orchid" metaphor into practice to identify which of your employees need more or less of your time and involvement, try to embrace your role as the gardener of this patch of contrary behavior.

To oversee and nurture this bouquet of diverse skills and potential, you must become a model of the behavior you're trying to evoke.

To that end, consider:

- Most managers, by virtue of their working their way up the organization's hierarchy to positions of authority, are weeds. That doesn't mean, however, that you'll never have an "orchid moment" or slip into the daisy patch; everyone who faces new challenges has to spend at least some time learning how to excel under the new conditions. Don't be afraid to admit it when it happens to you.

- Admitting that you need some temporary coaching will allow you to get it—and to work your way back to "weed speed" in no time. Enlist the support of your own managers, mentors, and colleagues whom you admire. Ask them to help you as you pursue your personal, continuous growth.

• Empower yourself to set limits when it comes to how much time and involvement you devote to each employee. Use the "weed, daisy, orchid" metaphor to identify your employees and to plan your time accordingly.

• Take responsibility for the consequences of allowing a career orchid to tangle the roots of the rest of the flowers in your garden. If you don't have the nerve to terminate a problem employee, *you must be accountable for that inaction.* (Consider enlisting the support of another manager who can coach you on how to take the necessary action in a way that suits your conscience.)

• Above all, be fair to your employees. It's not fair to treat them all the same. Each flower has its own response to the sunlight you let into its environment—and to the shadows you cast when you ignore it. Same goes for your employees.

Now, pull on your gardening gloves and get to work!

How does *your* garden grow? It's up to you!

"One of the greatest discoveries a man
makes, one of his great surprises,
is to find he can do what he was
afraid he couldn't do."

—Henry Ford

Way To Grow!

A Closing Thought

Just as managers cannot empower their employees—
they can only create an environment that encourages
employees to empower themselves—only you can empower
yourself to be a good manager to your staff.

Just as an employee cannot self-empower without first
accepting responsibility for the outcome of the work—before
the fact—and being accountable for the consequences of his
or her own actions, you cannot empower yourself without
doing the same.

Apply the accountability scale to yourself. Do you claim
total responsibility for no less than 85 percent of your
own success—and blame no more than 15 percent of your
failures on factors beyond your control?

If so, you know that your employees do not make you a
good manager. Only you can do that.

As you accept the role of gardener to your plot of orchids,
daisies, and weeds, take stock of your own behaviors and
attitudes. Only an empowered person can preside over the
Garden of Empowerment.

Be that person. Be a *weed*.

Way To Grow!

About the Author

Linda Galindo is one of the most dynamic and knowledgeable organizational consultants on the scene today. As founder and president of Galindo Consulting Inc., Galindo has earned the trust and deep respect of CEOs, executives, and managers for her ability to facilitate the development of high-performance teams. She delivers direct, solid management consulting content, along with a dynamic, engaging presentation style.

With 15 years of experience in cultural competence, change management, leadership development, and cultural assessment to her credit, Galindo is welcomed into every aspect of organizational development. Additionally, her work in creating cultures of accountability and mutual respect is utilized in every level of organizations from the boardroom to information technology departments in multinational corporations.

A gifted keynote speaker, Galindo possesses enough energy and vitality to light up an auditorium for 90 minutes. Among her most popular presentations are: "The Power of What You Don't Know," "The Change Challenge" and "Lead, Follow, or Get Out of the Way!"

As an executive coach, she teaches executives how to develop the qualities that make better leaders. Her one-on-one program enables her clients to consistently uphold the business values their organizations hold dear. Galindo conducts seminars and retreats for hundreds of participants annually. Her most frequently requested seminars include: "Personal and Organizational High Performance," "High-Performance Accountability," "The Everyday Leader" and "From Gen-X to Geri-X: Working with Generational Differences in the Workplace."

WALK THE TALK®
Presentations & Workshops

Bring Linda Galindo and her powerful message to your organization through our high-impact:

- Keynote & Conference Presentations
- Leadership Development Workshops
- Train-The-Trainer/Certification Services

WALK THE TALK Presentations and Workshops are customized to your audience, organizational culture, and targeted business objectives. Our cadre of experienced authors and facilitators are dedicated to providing you with a powerful educational experience, to help you ensure the complete success of your sponsored event.

We offer educational programs and presentations on each topic covered in our best-selling books to include:

- Effective Leadership Techniques
- Business Ethics and Values Alignment
- Coaching and Performance Improvement Strategies
- Building Customer Service Attitudes and Behaviors
- Techniques to Attract and Retain "The Best and Brightest Employees"
- Building a High-Performance Culture
- Dealing With Organizational Change
- *And much, much more*

To learn more:
Call 972.243.8863 or toll free 1.800.888.2811
or
E-mail info@walkthetalk.com

The WALK THE TALK Leadership Development Library

Only $99.95!

Contains 13 of our best-selling WALK THE TALK publications. When you place your order for *Way To Grow!*, be sure to include The WALK THE TALK Leadership Development Library!

The WALK THE TALK Company

Since 1977, **The WALK THE TALK® Company** has helped organizations, worldwide, achieve success through Ethical Leadership and Values-Based Business Practices. And our team of experienced professionals is ready to do the same ... for YOU!

We offer the following professional resources:
- Keynote and Conference Presentations
- Customized Workshops
- Executive Retreats
- Consulting Services
- "How To" Handbooks
- Video Training Packages
- *and much more!*

To learn more:	
Call:	1.888.822.9255
E-mail:	info@walkthetalk.com
Visit:	www.walkthetalk.com

Four easy ways to order

Way to Grow!

and

The Leadership Development Library

ONLINE

www.walkthetalk.com
Visit our website 24 hours a day

FAX

972.243.0815

MAIL

The WALK THE TALK Company
2925 LBJ Freeway, Suite 201
Dallas, TX 75234

or

PHONE

1.888.822.9255 (Toll Free), or 972.243.8863
Monday through Friday, 8:30 a.m.–5 p.m., Central

The WALK THE TALK® Company

Helping organizations achieve success through Ethical
Leadership and Values-Based Business Practices

ORDER FORM
Have questions? Need assistance? *Call 1.888.822.9255*

 Please send me more copies of *Way To Grow!*
1–24 copies $12.95 each   25–99 copies $11.95 each   100–499 copies $10.95 each   500+ copies, *please call*

✔ **Please send me The Leadership Development Library**
$99.95 per set

Way To Grow! _____ copies X _____ = $_____

Leadership Development Library _____ sets X _____ = $_____

Client Priority Code	Product Total $_____
	*Shipping & Handling $_____
	Subtotal $_____

Sales & Use Tax Collected on TX & CA Customers Only)

Sales Tax:
Texas Sales Tax–8.25% $_____

CA Sales/Use Tax $_____

Total (U.S. Dollars Only) $_____

*Shipping and Handling Charges

No. of items	1–4	5–9	10–24	25–49	50–99	100–199	200+
Total Shipping	$6.75	$10.95	$17.95	$26.95	$48.95	$84.95	$89.95+$0.25/book

Call 972.243.8863 for quote if outside the continental U.S. • Orders are shipped ground delivery 7–10 days. Next and 2nd business day delivery available — call 1.888.822.9255.

Name _____ Title_____

Organization _____

Shipping Address _____

City _____ No PO Boxes _____ State _____ Zip _____

E-mail _____

Charge Your Order: ❑ MasterCard ❑ Visa ❑ American Express

Credit Card Number _____ Exp. Date _____

❑ Check Enclosed (Payable to The WALK THE TALK Company)

❑ Please Invoice **(Orders over $250 ONLY)** ❑ P.O. Number *(if applicable)* _____

PHONE	**FAX**	**MAIL**
1.888.822.9255	972.243.0815	The WALK THE TALK Co.
or 972.243.8863.		2925 LBJ Fwy. #201
M–F, 8:30–5:00 Cen.	**ONLINE**	Dallas, TX 75234
	www.walkthetalk.com	

Prices effective December 2004 are subject to change.